ANCIENT GREEKS

AT A GLANCE

JOHN MALAM

PETER BEDRICK BOOKS
NEW YORK

Published by
PETER BEDRICK BOOKS
156 Fifth Avenue
New York, NY 10010

© Macdonald Young Books 1998
Text and illustrations © Macdonald Young Books

Edited by: Annie Scothern
Series editor: Lisa Edwards
Illustrated by: Maltings Partnership
Designed by: The Design Works, Reading, UK
Classical Greek consultant: Dr. Simon Goldhill, King's
College, Cambridge, UK

Library of Congress Cataloging-in-Publication Data
Malam, John.
Ancient Greeks at a glance / John Malam.
p. cm.
Includes index.
Summary: An illustrated survey of the society, culture, and
history of ancient Greece.
ISBN 0-87226-557-9
1. Greece--Civilization--To 146 B.C.--Juvenile literature.
2. Greeks--Social life and customs--Juvenile literature. 3.
Greece--History--To 146 B. C. --Juvenile literature. [1.
Greece--Civilization--To 146 B. C. 2. Greece--History--
To 146 B. C.]
I. Title.
DF79.M28 1998
938--dc21 98-11862
CIP
AC

Printed in Hong Kong by Wing King Tong
First American edition, 1998

CONTENTS

TIME TRACK

The time of the Ancient Greeks is divided into different ages – from the first people who lived in Greece up until the time Greece became part of the Roman Empire. About 8,500 years ago, the first farmers lived on the mainland of Greece and some nearby islands. They lived in small villages. Gradually, over hundreds of years, the Ancient Greeks began to make important changes to their way of life. Ancient Greek civilization had started to appear, and it flourished from then onwards. ▼

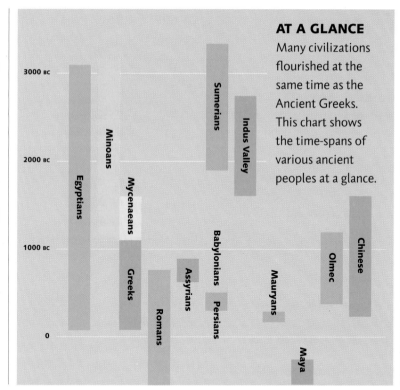

AT A GLANCE
Many civilizations flourished at the same time as the Ancient Greeks. This chart shows the time-spans of various ancient peoples at a glance.

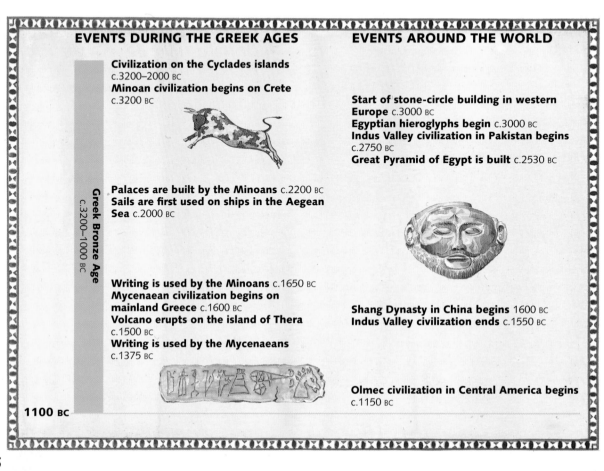

EVENTS DURING THE GREEK AGES

Greek Bronze Age c.3200–1000 BC

Civilization on the Cyclades islands c.3200–2000 BC
Minoan civilization begins on Crete c.3200 BC

Palaces are built by the Minoans c.2200 BC
Sails are first used on ships in the Aegean Sea c.2000 BC

Writing is used by the Minoans c.1650 BC
Mycenaean civilization begins on mainland Greece c.1600 BC
Volcano erupts on the island of Thera c.1500 BC
Writing is used by the Mycenaeans c.1375 BC

1100 BC

EVENTS AROUND THE WORLD

Start of stone-circle building in western Europe c.3000 BC
Egyptian hieroglyphs begin c.3000 BC
Indus Valley civilization in Pakistan begins c.2750 BC
Great Pyramid of Egypt is built c.2530 BC

Shang Dynasty in China begins 1600 BC
Indus Valley civilization ends c.1550 BC

Olmec civilization in Central America begins c.1150 BC

EVENTS DURING THE GREEK AGES

EVENTS AROUND THE WORLD

1100 BC

Dark Age c.1100–800 BC

Minoan civilization ends c.1100 BC
Mycenaean civilization ends c.1100 BC
First use of iron for tools and weapons
c.1100 BC

Shang Dynasty ends 1027 BC

**Some Greeks flee the mainland and settle
on Aegean islands** c.1050–950 BC

900 BC

First Olympic Games are held 776 BC
**Greeks begin to establish colonies
overseas** c.750 BC
First Greek alphabet is used c.750 BC

City of Rome is founded 753 BC

700 BC

Archaic Age c.800–500 BC

Trade with Egypt and Africa c.660–630 BC
Black-figure pottery is made c.610 BC
First Greek coins are used c.600 BC

Coinage is invented in Lydia (Turkey) c.625 BC

The Buddha is born in India 563 BC
Persian Empire is founded 550 BC

Red-figure pottery is made c.535 BC
Democracy is introduced in Athens c.505 BC

Roman Republic is founded 509 BC

500 BC

Classical Age c.500–323 BC

Piraeus becomes the port of Athens 493 BC
Wars against the Persians 490–480 BC
Parthenon at Athens built 447–432 BC
Athens and Sparta at war 431–404 BC
Philip II becomes king of Macedonia 359 BC
Theater at Epidauros built 358–330 BC
**Philip II dies and Alexander the Great
becomes king of Macedonia** 336 BC
Conquests of Alexander the Great 334–323 BC
Alexander the Great dies 323 BC

The Buddha dies 486 BC

Celts attack Rome 390 BC

Rome conquers Italy 334–264 BC

300 BC

Hellenistic Age 323–30 BC

Invasion by Gauls 279 BC

First Roman coins are used c.280 BC

Hannibal defeats a Roman army 218 BC
Great Wall of China is built 214 BC

Macedonia becomes a Roman province
148 BC
**Mainland Greece becomes a Roman
province** 146 BC
Greek cities overseas pass to the Romans
129 BC

100 BC

**Egypt, the last of the Hellenistic (Greek)
kingdoms, becomes a Roman province** 30 BC

0

7

SITE-SEEING –
A GUIDE TO ANCIENT GREECE

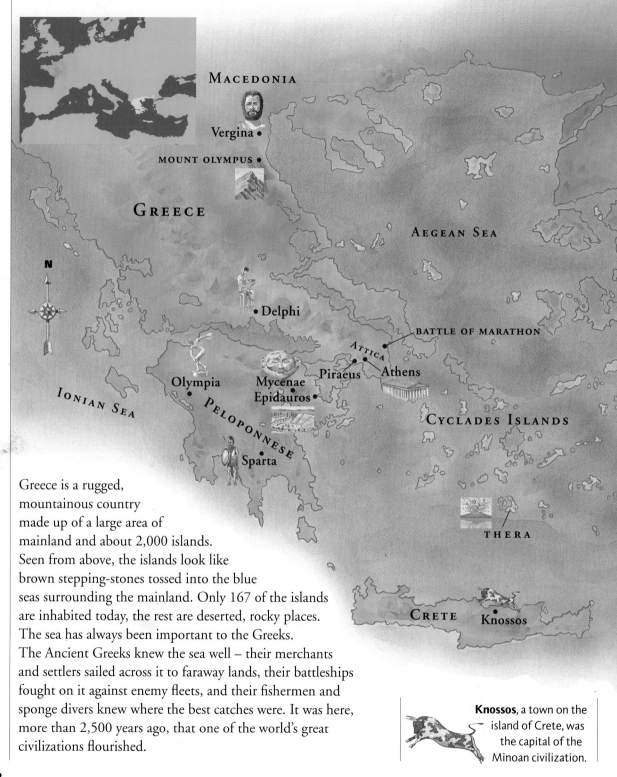

MACEDONIA

Vergina •

MOUNT OLYMPUS •

GREECE

AEGEAN SEA

N

• Delphi

BATTLE OF MARATHON

ATTICA

Olympia •

Mycenae

Piraeus •

Athens

Epidauros •

IONIAN SEA

PELOPONNESE

CYCLADES ISLANDS

Sparta •

THERA

CRETE

Knossos •

Greece is a rugged,
mountainous country
made up of a large area of
mainland and about 2,000 islands.
Seen from above, the islands look like
brown stepping-stones tossed into the blue
seas surrounding the mainland. Only 167 of the islands
are inhabited today, the rest are deserted, rocky places.
The sea has always been important to the Greeks.
The Ancient Greeks knew the sea well – their merchants
and settlers sailed across it to faraway lands, their battleships
fought on it against enemy fleets, and their fishermen and
sponge divers knew where the best catches were. It was here,
more than 2,500 years ago, that one of the world's great
civilizations flourished.

Knossos, a town on the
island of Crete, was
the capital of the
Minoan civilization.

Macedonia, in the far north, was always thought of as an out-of-the-way place. Its name came from a word meaning 'highlanders'. It was the home of the powerful Philip II and his son, Alexander the Great.

Vergina was where Macedonian rulers were buried, including Philip II.

Olympia was the giant sports complex where the Olympic Games festival was held. This was the most important Greek festival and took place every four years in honor of the god Zeus. The statue of Zeus at Olympia was one of the Seven Wonders of the Ancient World.

Peloponnese is the jagged-shaped peninsula in the south. It is joined to the rest of the mainland by a strip of land only 7 miles wide. Its name means 'island of Pelops'. Pelops was a prince in a Greek story. Ancient Greek civilization began in this part of Greece.

M E D I T E R R A N E A N   S E A

Mycenae was one of the first Greek cities. In later times it was remembered as a city 'rich in gold'.

Sparta was little more than a group of powerful villages built around a central hill. It became the chief Greek city for a short time after it won a war against Athens. The Spartan army was the bravest of all the Greek armies.

Mount Olympus is the tallest mountain on mainland Greece (9,570 feet). The Greeks believed it was the home of their gods and goddesses.

Delphi was thought to be the very center of the world. One of the most important temples in Greece was here.

Attica was the territory of Athens. Among its hills were areas of good farming land, as well as valuable sources of silver, marble and clay. These all helped to make Athens rich.

Marathon was the site of a famous battle. A small Greek army defeated a much larger army from Persia here, saving Athens from being attacked.

Athens became the most important city in Greece. The idea of democracy ('power by the people') began here. The famous Parthenon temple was built on the hill above the city.

Piraeus is the main port of Athens. It is over 4 miles from the city.

Epidauros was a center of healing where sick people went to be cured. It was also the site of a large theater.

Thera (or **Santorini**), an island in the Aegean Sea, was inhabited by people rather like the Minoans. A volcanic eruption in about 1500 BC blew the island in half. A later Greek story about the lost island of Atlantis may have been based on the destruction of Thera.

BEFORE THE GREEKS WERE THE MINOANS

The Minoans lived on Crete. Their civilization lasted for about 2,000 years. They were not Greeks, but their story is part of the history of Ancient Greece. The archaeologist who first uncovered their towns and palaces called them Minoans, after King Minos, who was said to have lived on Crete long ago. Minoans were farmers and fishers, and they knew how to write.

MYCENAEANS – THE FIRST GREEKS

The Mycenaeans were traders and warriors, ruled over by kings. They lived in small kingdoms on the Greek mainland. Their towns were protected by strong walls, as if they were castles. The Mycenaeans learned the art of writing from the Minoans. The Mycenaean and Minoan civilizations ended at the same time. Hundreds of years later, the Ancient Greeks remembered the Mycenaeans as a race of heroes.

This gold mask was found in a grave at Mycenae. It shows the face of a Mycenaean man.

TRADE, TRAVEL AND FARMING

TRADING AS A WAY OF LIFE

The Ancient Greeks were the greatest traders of their time. The sea was their link to faraway places, and they traded around the Mediterranean and beyond. The first Greek traders bartered for goods, but later on they used coins (money) to pay for them. They traded for raw materials that could not be found in Greece (such as tin), for food (especially grain such as wheat) and for luxury goods that could be sold for high prices at home (such as ivory).

OVERSEAS COLONIES

The population of Greece increased after about the year 800 BC. Because farmland was in short supply, farmers found it hard to grow enough food to feed all the people. The Greeks found a good way of solving this problem. Some people left Greece and went to live in other lands around the Mediterranean coast, where they built new towns. These towns were colonies, and each one belonged to a 'mother-city' in Greece. The colonies sent food and trade goods back to their hungry mother-cities.

The Greeks built so many cities in southern Italy and Sicily that they nicknamed the area 'Greater Greece'. The Greeks went to Italy to farm the open countryside and to trade with the people who lived there. ▼

The area that became known as 'Greater Greece'

• Some Greek colonies (these are their Greek names)

IMPORTS AND EXPORTS

The Greeks were keen to buy goods from other countries (imports). ▼

Copper from **Cyprus** and **Spain**

Grain from the **Black Sea** area (south **Russia**), **Egypt**, **Cyprus**, **Italy** and **Sicily**

Amber from **Denmark** and lands around the **Baltic Sea**

Lead from **Italy**

Ivory from **Egypt** and **North Africa**

Papyrus (a kind of paper) from **Egypt**

Textiles from **Egypt**

Silver ore from **Italy**

Olive oil from **Cyprus** and **North Africa**

Tin from **Italy**, the **East** and **Britain**

Timber from **Cyprus** and **Italy**

Greeks also had valuable goods of their own to sell abroad (exports). ▼

Pottery

Honey

Olive oil

Silver ore

Slaves

Wine

TRAVEL AND TRANSPORT

Roads in Ancient Greece were often no better than dusty tracks. When people traveled cross-country they either walked or rode on donkeys. For longer journeys people used horse-drawn carriages. These were big enough to carry passengers and their goods.

But if a journey could be made by sea, then that was how people preferred to travel. The best time for sea travel was between May and September, when the water was calm. Only the bravest seafarers traveled in autumn and winter.

Sea travel was fast – merchants' ships could sail up to 10 miles a day, taking people and goods to and from cities in Greece and the colonies overseas. A merchant ship was made from timber and had one square sail.
If the wind didn't blow it along, it could be rowed.

FARMING THE LAND AND FISHING THE SEA

Farmers were the most respected of all Greek workers because it was their job to provide food for the people. They grew barley, wheat, olives, grapes, apples, pears, figs, pomegranates, peas and green beans. Crops such as potatoes and tomatoes were unknown in Greece at this time. Flax was grown for weaving into linen, and millet was grown to feed animals. Farmers kept sheep, goats, cattle, pigs and bees.

◀ Olives were very important to the Ancient Greeks. Apart from eating the olives, the Greeks squashed them and collected the oil that came out. This was used for cooking, washing, as lamp fuel and as a treatment for injured athletes. The olive harvest was gathered in September.

KEY
1 men knocked the olives down with sticks
2 women and girls picked up the olives from the ground
3 boys climbed the trees to reach the olives at the top

The sea provided a never-ending supply of fish – from sardines and swordfish to octopus and squid. Divers gathered sponges from the seabed. People used sponges for washing themselves. ▼

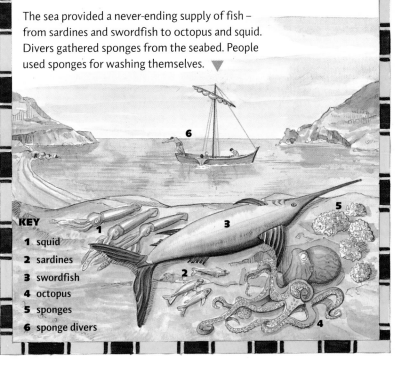

KEY
1 squid
2 sardines
3 swordfish
4 octopus
5 sponges
6 sponge divers

GREAT GREEKS

The Ancient Greeks loved life and wanted to know all about it. They were hungry for knowledge. Not only did they want to find out *how* things worked, they also wanted to find out *why* things were the way they were. Because of this constant searching they made many great discoveries, some of which have helped to make the world the way it is today.

Aristotle (384–322 BC) lived for much of his life in Athens. He is famous because he divided things into separate science subjects, such as biology, zoology and physics. We study the same subjects today. Aristotle believed that science should be based on observations and experiments. He taught the young Alexander, who became the conquering general, Alexander the Great (see page 20).

When Alexander conquered lands far away from Greece he found new plants and animals. He sent these to Aristotle for him to study.

EUREKA!

Archimedes (C.287–212 BC) was one of the greatest mathematicians of all time. He was born in the Greek colony of Syracuse, on the island of Sicily. He worked out ways of measuring circles, and he discovered how levers can be used to lift heavy objects.

Archimedes' most famous discovery came when he was having a bath. He had been asked to work out if a gold crown had any false gold in it. He had noticed how his bath water had overflowed when he climbed in. This is called 'displacement' – where an object will always displace (move) its own volume in water. Archimedes realized that a crown of solid gold would displace more water than a crown with false gold in it. He was so pleased with his discovery that he ran naked through the streets shouting '*Eureka!*', which means 'I have found it!' in Greek.

Hippocrates (c.460–390 BC) ran a school of medicine on the island of Cos. He trained doctors, teaching them how to care for patients by understanding the symptoms (signs) of their illness. His students took an oath (a promise) before they were allowed to work as doctors. Part of the Hippocratic Oath said: 'I will use treatment to help the sick… I will not give poison to anyone'.

Eratosthenes (c.275–194 BC) was in charge of the famous Library in the Greek city of Alexandria, in Egypt. He knew about astronomy, mathematics and philosophy. Most of all, he discovered things about geography. He realized that all the oceans were one. He worked out the distance around the Earth, calculating it to within 200 miles of the actual distance (24,900 miles). This was a great achievement for someone living so long ago.

Plato (c.427–347 BC) lived and worked in Athens, where he founded a school for thinking known as the Academy. He had ideas about how to make the world a better place. Students studied his teachings at the Academy for 1,000 years until the Romans closed it down.

Socrates (469–399 BC) was the greatest thinker of his day. His teachings were so important that they are still in use. He looked for the truth about things by asking questions such as: 'What is beautiful and what is ugly?' Questions like this are hard to answer because they make people ask themselves why they think and behave the way they do.

WHY ARE THEY FAMOUS?

Homer (c.850–750 BC) a poet

Homer

500 BC

Sophocles (c.496–406 BC) a playwright who wrote tragedies

Pericles (c.495–429 BC) a statesman from Athens whose idea it was to build the Parthenon

Herodotus (c.484–425 BC) an historian who wrote about the wars with the Persians and is sometimes called the 'Father of History'

Socrates (469–399 BC) a philosopher who thought about truth

Phidias (worked c.460–430 BC) the greatest sculptor of Ancient Greece, whose statues decorated the Parthenon at Athens and the temple of Zeus at Olympia

Hippocrates (c.460–390 BC) a doctor

Aristophanes (c.450–c.385 BC) a playwright who wrote comedies

Plato (c.427–347 BC) a philosopher who thought about goodness, beauty and justice

400 BC

Aristotle (384–322 BC) a philosopher and scientist

Philip II (c.382–336 BC) a Macedonian king and military leader

Alexander the Great (356–323 BC) a Macedonian king and military leader whose conquests gained an empire for Greece

Aristarchus (c.310–c.230 BC) a mathematician and astronomer who believed the Earth revolved around the Sun

300 BC

Archimedes (c.287–212 BC) a mathematician

Eratosthenes (c.275–194 BC) an astronomer, mathematician and philosopher, and one of the cleverest of the Ancient Greeks

GREEK SOCIETY

There were two distinct sides to Ancient Greek society. On the 'fair' side ordinary people were given a say in how they wanted things done. On the 'unfair' side people such as women and foreigners were treated as second-class citizens, and slaves led a life that could be tough and cruel. It was as if some Greeks were thought of as being 'more Greek' than others.

GOVERNMENT

The Ancient Greeks invented a form of government called 'democracy', or 'power by the people'. The idea was to allow people to vote for how they wanted their city to be run. It was the people who had the power to pass laws, elect officials, declare war and make peace. Only men over the age of eighteen who were born in the city, or its surrounding territory, could vote. Women, slaves and foreigners could not vote. ▶

Democracy was invented in Athens. Men who could vote held a meeting, or an 'assembly', on a hill in the city called the Pnyx (see page 22). After listening to speakers, the men voted for what they wanted by raising their hands in a hand-count.

PUNISHMENT BY DEMOCRACY

If the citizens of Athens disliked a person, they could throw him out of the city. Once a year a vote was held in the Agora (see page 23). More than 6,000 people had to take part, otherwise the vote would not be allowed. This was democracy in action – letting ordinary citizens make decisions.

When Athenians voted to send someone away from Athens, they scratched the person's name on pieces of pottery called *ostraka*, from which we get the word 'ostracize' (banish). The person with the most votes had to leave Athens for ten years. This one says 'Kimon, son of Miltiades'.

CITY-STATES

Ancient Greece was a collection of small units called 'city-states'. A city-state was a city and the territory around it. Each city-state had its own government, its own laws and its own coins. There was no single system for the whole country. Some city-states fought each other, as Athens and Sparta did. Others were friends and supported one another. The Greeks called each city-state a *polis*, from which we get the word 'politics'.

MONEY

Coins were invented in Lydia (modern-day Turkey) in about 625 BC. The Lydians were neighbors of the Greeks. Coins were easy to carry and store, and most of all they could be counted. The idea caught on and soon the Greeks were making and using their own coins. Most Greek coins were made from solid silver. They were made to standard weights and sizes so that people would know how much the coins were worth. Each Greek city made its own coins, stamped with its own designs.

A silver coin from Athens showing the city's patron goddess Athena on the front and an owl, with which she was linked, on the back. The letters spell part of her name: 'ATHE'. This is the actual size of the coin.

SLAVES

The Ancient Greeks had slaves. Aristotle (see page 12) said a slave was 'a living tool'. A slave was 'owned' by a person. Slaves had no rights. It was their job to work for their owners, who fed and clothed them. People were made into slaves if they were captured in wars. Male slaves did the most dangerous work, such as working in mines. Women and children worked as servants in people's homes. They were slaves too.

CHILDREN AND EDUCATION

When a baby was born, the parents were pleased if it was a boy. Boys were seen as more 'useful' to their parents than girls. A boy would one day own property and inherit his father's land. A girl could not do this. Boys went to school from the age of seven to eighteen. They learned how to read, write, count, play music and take part in games such as gymnastics. Girls stayed at home, where they learned the basics of reading, writing, counting, and most of all, how to weave and work with wool.

A teacher giving a young boy a grammar lesson.

WOMEN

Women and men were not equal. Women were not allowed to own much property. They could not vote or take part in politics. A woman had to look after children, clean, weave and do household chores. It was only at times of religious festivals that women were allowed to take a greater part in society, and some became priestesses in temples. Women married at the age of twelve or fourteen and had an average of four children.

Ancient Greeks thought that a woman's place was in the home. This woman is putting folded sheets into a chest, keeping the house neat and tidy.

Everyday Life

CLOTHES, HAIRSTYLES AND JEWELRY

Men, women and children wore a basic loose-fitting garment, which was called a *chiton*. Clothes (usually of wool or linen) were made at home by women and female servants. Women wore make-up and gold jewelry and arranged their hair into lots of different styles.

KEY

1 a woman's chiton hung from her shoulders and fell to the ground
2 her long hair was tied up with ribbon
3 she used white make-up on her face – pale skin was thought to be more attractive than dark skin
4 a belt held her chiton at the waist
5 she also wore a *himation* – a cloak that went over her chiton
6 dangling gold earrings, necklaces and bracelets were always popular
7 mirrors were made from polished bronze

8 a working man wore a short, knee-length chiton
9 a broad-rimmed hat protected him against the hot sun
10 he kept his hair short and had a neatly trimmed beard
11 on a long walk he wore lace-up leather boots

FOOD AND FEASTING

Ordinary people ate barley bread and cakes, and porridge made from mixed grains. If they could afford to, people also ate cheese, fish, fruit and vegetables. At a feast, rich Greeks might have fish, eels or quail (small birds) with vegetables cooked and served in savory sauces or in sauces sweetened with honey. (The Ancient Greeks used honey as we use sugar.) This was followed by fruit, nuts, cheese and honey cakes, washed down with lots of wine. Meat was only eaten in small quantities. Servants brought the food to the table, where it was eaten with the fingers.

WINE-MAKING AND DRINKING

The wines made by the Ancient Greeks had more alcohol in them than today's wines, which meant they were stronger. The Greeks mixed water with their wine. They thought it was unhealthy to drink undiluted wine, but wine mixed with water was said to be as good as medicine! ▶

CRAFTS

Vases were made in many shapes. On black-figure vases, the scene was painted in black while the background remained the color of the clay (red). ▶

On red-figure vases, the background was painted black so that the scene in red clay stood out. ▶

Statues were made from stone (marble) and from metal (bronze). Marble ones were brightly painted. The colors wore away over the years. ▶

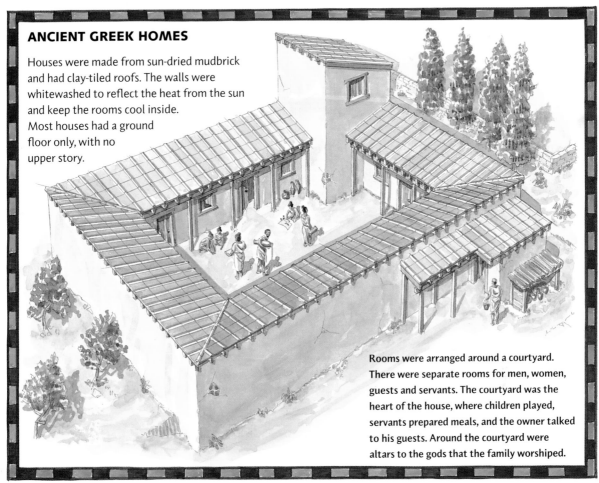

ANCIENT GREEK HOMES

Houses were made from sun-dried mudbrick and had clay-tiled roofs. The walls were whitewashed to reflect the heat from the sun and keep the rooms cool inside. Most houses had a ground floor only, with no upper story.

Rooms were arranged around a courtyard. There were separate rooms for men, women, guests and servants. The courtyard was the heart of the house, where children played, servants prepared meals, and the owner talked to his guests. Around the courtyard were altars to the gods that the family worshiped.

1 Ripe grapes were picked in September. Some were kept for eating. Workers trod on the rest to squeeze the juice out. The skins, pips and stalks were squeezed again in presses.

2 The juice was stored in tubs while it fermented (formed alcohol). In March, the wine was poured through cloth sieves to catch the bits. It was kept in large pottery jars called *pithoi*.

3 At the table, wine and water were mixed together in a large pot called a *krater*. The mixture was then ladled into pottery wine cups with handles, ready for drinking.

17

RELIGION

The Ancient Greeks thought their gods looked like ordinary people, but had extraordinary powers. The gods were stronger, braver and smarter than mere mortals, and were there to guide people in everything they did. People imagined their gods were watching over them all the time.

OLYMPIANS VERSUS TITANS

The most important gods were the twelve Olympian gods and goddesses. The Ancient Greeks believed that these gods lived on Mount Olympus, from which the group got its name. Zeus became the ruler of the Olympians after leading his fellow gods in a ten-year war against the old gods, called the Titans. The defeated Titans (except Atlas) were chained together and cast into the Underworld, where they faced never-ending torment in Tartarus.

Zeus used thunderbolts to defeat the Titans, and he punished Atlas by making him carry the world on his shoulders.

SACRIFICES TO PLEASE THE GODS

A Greek proverb said: 'Gifts persuade the gods'. This tells us a lot about how the Greeks practiced their religion. Food gifts for the gods were left on altars. The best gift was an animal. A bull was the greatest; a sheep was the most common.

The animal was led to the altar in a procession. Music was played and grains of barley were scattered. The animal was killed, cooked and eaten at a feast. Its bones were burned on the altar, the smoke rising to the god above.

THE TWELVE OLYMPIAN GODS AT A GLANCE

Aphrodite, goddess of love and beauty

Apollo, god of the sun, truth, music, poetry, dance and healing

Ares, god of war

Artemis, goddess of the moon, wild animals and childbirth

Athena, goddess of war, wisdom and art

Demeter, goddess of grain and fertility

Dionysus, god of wine and vegetation

Hephaestus, god of fire, volcanoes, blacksmiths and craftsmen

Hera, goddess of women and marriage

Hermes, god of travel, business, weights, measures and sports

Poseidon, god of the sea, earthquakes and horses

Zeus, god of the weather and ruler of the gods

TELLING THE FUTURE

The Ancient Greeks believed they could talk to the gods. At the famous temple of Apollo in Delphi, a male pilgrim would ask a priestess a question he wanted the gods to answer. She would go into a trance, then speak mysterious words. A male priest made sense of the words and wrote them down. This was the gods' answer to the pilgrim's question. It was the Greek equivalent of fortune-telling.

FUNERAL CUSTOMS

A dead person was buried as soon as possible. The body was washed and dressed, then carried on a stretcher to the burial ground. There it was put inside a wooden coffin or a stone sarcophagus (this comes from a Greek word meaning 'flesh-eater'). A coin was placed in its mouth. This was to pay Charon the ferryman. Food, drink and oil were left at the graveside and a tombstone was put on top of the grave.

TEMPLES FOR THE GODS

A temple was a home for a god or goddess to live in. The finest temples were built from white marble, painted in bright colors. The inside of the temple was a private place, from where a statue of the god looked out on the people worshiping at the sacrificial altar.

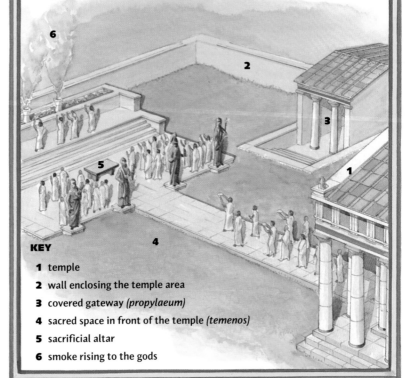

KEY

1. temple
2. wall enclosing the temple area
3. covered gateway *(propylaeum)*
4. sacred space in front of the temple *(temenos)*
5. sacrificial altar
6. smoke rising to the gods

THE GREEK AFTERLIFE

The Ancient Greeks believed in life after death. They believed in an Underworld ruled over by the god Hades. People who had led good lives went to live in a place of happiness called the Elysian Fields. Those who had been bad went to live in a place of eternal punishment called Tartarus. ▼

1 The god Hermes went with the dead person's spirit to the bank of the River Styx.

2 The River Styx was the boundary between the worlds of the living and the dead.

3 The dead paid Charon to row them across the river to the Underworld.

4 The entrance to the Underworld was guarded by a three-headed dog called Cerberus.

5 The Underworld became known as Hades, after the god who ruled it.

THE GREEKS AT WAR

The Ancient Greeks had different types of armies at various times in their history. The ones described here come from the time of King Philip II and his son, Alexander the Great, when the art of warfare was at its most advanced.

PHILIP II

Philip II was king of Macedonia, a kingdom in the north of Greece. He was a brilliant soldier and diplomat. He wanted to become ruler of all Greece. So he went to war against Athens and other Greek cities. In 338 BC his 30,000 soldiers defeated his enemies at the Battle of Chaeronea. Philip now controlled all of Greece. He began to plan a war against the Persians, the traditional enemies of the Greeks. But before he could act, he was murdered by one of his own nobles.

When Philip II's tomb was found, scientists used his skull to make a lifelike model of how he might have looked – including the arrow wound he is known to have had on his right eye.

ALEXANDER THE GREAT

Alexander was Philip II's son. He became king of Macedonia at the age of twenty, after his father died. He continued with Philip's plan to invade the vast Persian empire to the east of Greece. Within eleven years, 334–323 BC, Alexander's army had fought its way to India – defeating the Persian armies and winning an empire for Greece that was the greatest the world had ever known. Wherever he went Alexander built new cities, calling many of them 'Alexandria', after himself. His nickname 'Megas' meant 'the Great'. Alexander died aged only thirty-two, and his empire broke into separate parts (see page 28).

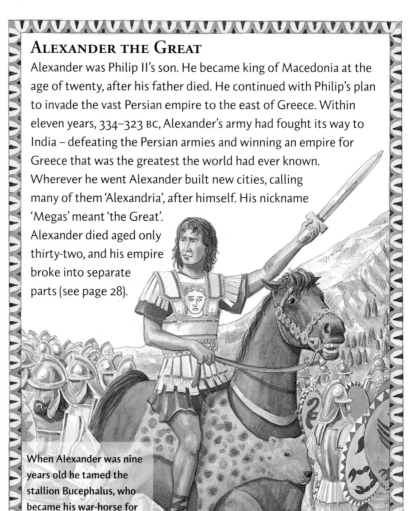

When Alexander was nine years old he tamed the stallion Bucephalus, who became his war-horse for the next twenty years.

PERSIA VERSUS GREECE

The Persians fought the Greeks many times. In 490 BC their leader Darius tried to take control of Greece. His army of 20,000 men landed at Marathon, 26 miles from Athens. In the battle that followed, the Persian invaders were defeated by just 9,000 Greek soldiers. Later, Darius' son Xerxes fought the Greeks at Salamis. The Persians lost, and their hopes of conquering Greece ended.

BIGGEST BATTLES

490 BC Battle of Marathon: Persian army defeated

480 BC Battle of Thermopylae: Greek army defeated

480 BC Battle of Salamis: Persian navy defeated

333 BC Battle of Issus: Persian army defeated by Alexander

331 BC Battle of Gaugamela: Persian army defeated by Alexander, who becomes the king of Persia

WAR ON LAND

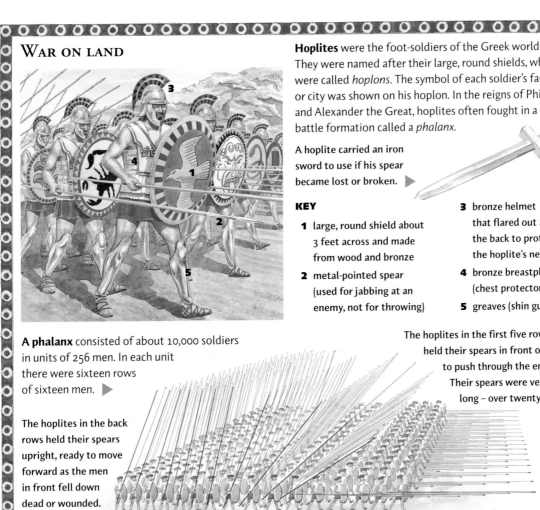

Hoplites were the foot-soldiers of the Greek world. They were named after their large, round shields, which were called *hoplons*. The symbol of each soldier's family or city was shown on his hoplon. In the reigns of Philip II and Alexander the Great, hoplites often fought in a battle formation called a *phalanx*.

A hoplite carried an iron sword to use if his spear became lost or broken. ▶

KEY

1 large, round shield about 3 feet across and made from wood and bronze

2 metal-pointed spear (used for jabbing at an enemy, not for throwing)

3 bronze helmet that flared out at the back to protect the hoplite's neck

4 bronze breastplate (chest protector)

5 greaves (shin guards)

A phalanx consisted of about 10,000 soldiers in units of 256 men. In each unit there were sixteen rows of sixteen men. ▶

The hoplites in the first five rows held their spears in front of them to push through the enemy. Their spears were very long – over twenty feet.

The hoplites in the back rows held their spears upright, ready to move forward as the men in front fell down dead or wounded.

■ Alexander's foot-soldiers

■ his cavalry

■ enemy foot- soldiers

◀ Soldiers on horseback (cavalry) rode in a wedge-shaped formation towards the enemy to create weak points where Greek foot-soldiers could attack.

◀ Some Greek armies used Indian elephants as 'living tanks' to frighten their enemies, especially their horses.

WAR AT SEA

The supreme fighting ship of the Greek navy was the *trireme*. It was powered by 170 oarsmen. The rowers sat in three rows, one above the other. Archers fired arrows at enemy ships from the flat deck.

A trireme had a bronze-covered post fitted to its prow so that it could ram and sink enemy ships.

THE CITY OF ATHENS

In the fifth century BC Athens became the foremost city of Ancient Greece. More than 200,000 people lived in the city and the surrounding countryside. Democracy began in Athens (see page 14); scientists, writers, poets and thinkers lived there; and visitors came from far and wide to marvel at the buildings on the hill above the city – just as they do today.

PIRAEUS, PORT OF ATHENS

The main port of Athens is 4 miles from the city. In ancient times Piraeus was home to the city's 200 warships. There were three harbors. Each harbor's entrance could be sealed by the raising of massive chains. Piraeus was a busy place where shipwrights built and repaired ships, and traders from all over the Greek world came to buy and sell goods.

Pericles (c.495–429 BC) was the great statesman and general who made Athens into a rich and beautiful city. He called it 'the greatest name in history… a power to be remembered forever'.

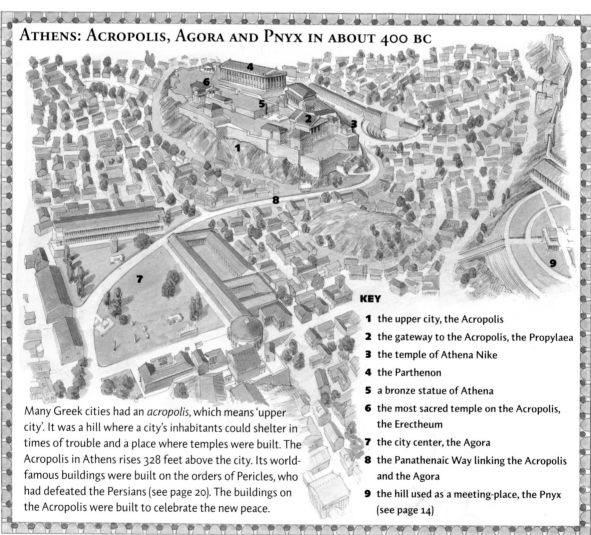

ATHENS: ACROPOLIS, AGORA AND PNYX IN ABOUT 400 BC

Many Greek cities had an *acropolis*, which means 'upper city'. It was a hill where a city's inhabitants could shelter in times of trouble and a place where temples were built. The Acropolis in Athens rises 328 feet above the city. Its world-famous buildings were built on the orders of Pericles, who had defeated the Persians (see page 20). The buildings on the Acropolis were built to celebrate the new peace.

KEY

1 the upper city, the Acropolis

2 the gateway to the Acropolis, the Propylaea

3 the temple of Athena Nike

4 the Parthenon

5 a bronze statue of Athena

6 the most sacred temple on the Acropolis, the Erectheum

7 the city center, the Agora

8 the Panathenaic Way linking the Acropolis and the Agora

9 the hill used as a meeting-place, the Pnyx (see page 14)

THE PARTHENON

The largest temple on the Acropolis is called the Parthenon. It was named after Athena Parthenos, the patron goddess of Athens, in whose honor it was built. It is said to be the most beautiful building to survive from ancient times. The Parthenon

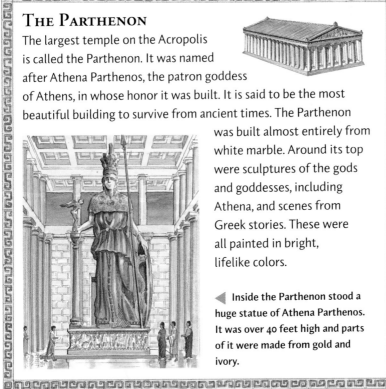

was built almost entirely from white marble. Around its top were sculptures of the gods and goddesses, including Athena, and scenes from Greek stories. These were all painted in bright, lifelike colors.

◀ Inside the Parthenon stood a huge statue of Athena Parthenos. It was over 40 feet high and parts of it were made from gold and ivory.

THE AGORA, THE CITY CENTER

The Agora was the center of social and business life. It was a large open square where every kind of thing could be bought – from pots and lamps to olive oil, fish and slaves. Temples, monuments and *stoas* stood around the Agora. A stoa was a long, narrow building with a roof held up by columns. It was open along one side so people could come and go as they pleased. A stoa offered shade in summer and shelter from rain in winter.

Merchants set up stalls inside the stoa. There were shops and offices at the back of the open-sided corridor.

ARCHITECTURAL 'ORDERS'

Greek buildings, especially temples, used columns to hold up the roof. Columns were made first from wood, then from stone and can be divided into three different styles, called 'orders':

Doric columns

Doric columns developed first.

1 The top of a column is called a capital. Doric capitals are plain.

2 Stone columns are made in sections, called drums. The grooves on the drums are called flutes. Each drum of a Doric column has twenty flutes.

3 Doric columns stand directly on the temple platform.

Ionic columns

1 Ionic capitals have a spiral scroll, called a volute, on two sides.

2 Each drum of an Ionic column has twenty-four flutes.

3 Ionic columns stand on a base on the temple platform.

Corinthian columns

Corinthian columns are similar to Ionic columns.

1 But their capitals have four sides decorated with carvings shaped like acanthus leaves.

Some of the columns in Ancient Greek buildings were made to look like people. Columns that look like women are called caryatids. This is one of six caryatids that hold up the south porch of the Erectheum. ▶

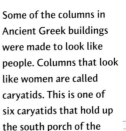

WRITING, MYTHS AND STORYTELLING

Being able to write is a sign of being civilized. The first Greeks who could write were the Mycenaeans (see page 9). But when the Mycenaean civilization ended, people stopped writing for about 350 years until the Greeks discovered the alphabet.

▲ The Mycenaeans used writing and picture signs like these 600 years before the Greeks learned about the alphabet from the Phoenicians.

THE GREEK ALPHABET

The alphabet was invented by the Phoenicians. They lived in the Middle East, where the countries of Lebanon and Syria are today. Greek merchants saw how useful the alphabet was for keeping records, so they borrowed the idea and took it back to Greece. In about 750 BC the first Greek alphabet appeared. It was a great success because it was easy to learn, and it spread quickly to all parts of the Greek world.

WHAT THEY WROTE ON

Ancient Greeks wrote mainly on scrolls made from pieces of papyrus glued into rolls. Papyrus was a type of early paper made from a water plant that grew in Egypt, which is where Greek merchants bought it.

A writing scroll made from papyrus could be over 30 feet long. The Greeks called it a *biblion*, from which we get the word 'bible'.

Classical Greek Alphabet		Latin Alphabet
Name	Letter	Letter
Alpha	A	A
Beta	B	B
Gamma	Γ	C/G
Delta	Δ	D
Epsilon	E	E
Digamma	F	F
Zeta	Z	Z
Eta	H	H
Theta	Θ	Th
Iota	I	I/J
Kappa	K	K
Lambda	Λ	L
Mu	M	M
Nu	N	N
Xi	Ξ	X
Omicron	O	O
Pi	Π	P
Qoppa	Ϙ	Q
Rho	P	R
Sigma	Σ	S
Tau	T	T
Upsilon	Υ	U/V
Phi	Φ	Ph
Chi	X	Ch
Psi	Ψ	Ps
Omega	Ω	Ō

▲ The twenty-six letters of the Ancient Greek alphabet as they looked in 500 BC. The word 'alphabet' comes from the names of the first two Greek letters, *alpha* and *beta*.

SECRET MESSAGES

During the war between Athens and Sparta (see page 9), the Spartans had a clever way of writing secret messages.

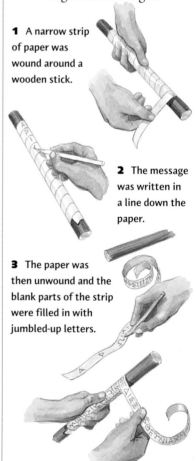

1 A narrow strip of paper was wound around a wooden stick.

2 The message was written in a line down the paper.

3 The paper was then unwound and the blank parts of the strip were filled in with jumbled-up letters.

4 The message could only be read by someone who had a stick that was the same thickness as the original one. When the strip was twisted around the stick, the letters lined up and the message reappeared.

HOMER, THE POET

Homer was the earliest and greatest Greek poet. He is thought to have lived at the time of the first Greek alphabet, in the eighth century BC.

No one knows what Homer looked like. He may have been blind. His epic poems, the *Iliad* and the *Odyssey*, are about Greek heroes who fought a war against the city of Troy, in present-day Turkey. This was called the Trojan War.

BARDS

Bards (storytellers) recited or sang stories and poems at public meetings. In Greece, bards were known as *rhapsoidoi* ('song-stitchers'). Their skill was in telling a well-known story in a new way, literally 'stitching' it together as they went along, without changing its meaning.

A bard spoke or sang in a flowing rhythm, which made his story more interesting to listen to. ▶

GREEK MYTHS

The Greeks loved stories, especially ones about their heroes and events from the past. Some of these events are based on true things that happened long ago, but like all good stories many of them are made up. We call all these stories 'myths'.

◀ This is a scene from the myth of Theseus and the Minotaur. Theseus was a Greek hero. He killed a beast called the Minotaur, who had the head of a bull and the body of a man. The beast lived in a maze, called the Labyrinth, on the island of Crete. According to the myth, fourteen young people were fed to the Minotaur every nine years. Theseus set out to kill the beast. He was helped by Ariadne, who gave him a ball of magic wool. Theseus unravelled it as he walked through the maze. After killing the Minotaur, Theseus found his way out of the Labyrinth by following the trail of wool.

Sports, Music and Theater

Sports and festivals

To the Greeks, sports was an important part of life, especially for boys and men. Sports helped to develop a boy's character, teaching him about winning and losing as well as making his body stronger. The Ancient Greeks thought that sports and religion were connected, which is why festivals often mixed the two together. Most sporting contests were for men only. However, in the city-state of Sparta there were gymnastic contests for girls.

THE OLYMPIC GAMES

The Olympic Games were held at Olympia every four years, in honor of the chief god Zeus. Men came from all over the Greek world to compete in the games. The Olympic Games festival was also the most important religious festival of all.

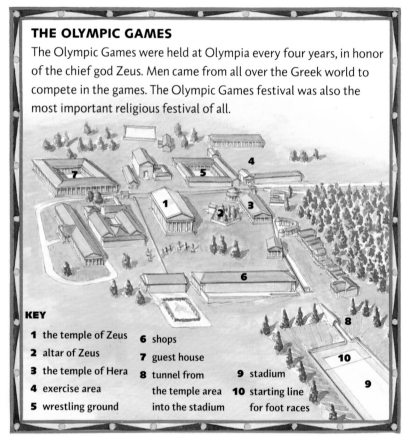

KEY

1 the temple of Zeus
2 altar of Zeus
3 the temple of Hera
4 exercise area
5 wrestling ground

6 shops
7 guest house
8 tunnel from the temple area into the stadium

9 stadium
10 starting line for foot races

PROGRAM OF EVENTS AT THE OLYMPIC GAMES

Athletes went to Olympia a month before the festival to train and prepare themselves. The five-day festival was held in August or September. All wars between Greek cities were suspended while the games were in progress. ▼

Day 1 – a day of sacrifices to the gods and the time when athletes swore to use only fair means to win

Day 2 – chariot-race, horse-race and pentathlon (foot-race, long jump, discus, javelin, wrestling)

Day 3 – the great day of the festival when 100 oxen were sacrificed to Zeus in the morning, followed by sporting contests for boys in the afternoon

Day 4 – foot-races, wrestling, boxing, *pankration* (a mixture of boxing, kicking and wrestling) and, last of all, the race in armor

Day 5 – a day of feasting and rejoicing

The Greeks admired strength and beauty, and athletes trained hard to build up their bodies so they could show them off at contests. In most games male athletes competed naked, or nearly so. ▼

Athletes in a foot-race ran a set number of lengths along a straight track.

An athlete swung two weights to help himself go further in the long jump.

This athlete is throwing the *discos* (discus), a disk of metal or stone.

Inside the temple of Zeus at Olympia was one of the Seven Wonders of the Ancient World. It was a statue of Zeus, 40 feet high and made from wood, ivory and gold. On a nearby altar burned a fire that was never allowed to go out.

MUSIC AND SONG

Greek music was closely related to poetry. Bards spoke or sang poems, making their words flow like music (see page 25). Musicians were often female. They sang songs and played instruments at feasts and festivals.

The *lyre* was a stringed instrument played by plucking. It was played slowly and its sound was soothing.

The *aulos* was a wind instrument like a flute. It was played quickly to make shrill, exciting sounds to dance to.

THEATER AND PLAYS

Every major Greek city had an open-air theater for the performance of plays. These took place during the day, not at night. Two particular types of play developed in Athens, called 'tragedy' and 'comedy'. A tragedy was a serious play based on a well-known myth (see page 25). A comedy was funny and could even be rude. Actors dressed in costumes and wore masks to show that their character was happy or sad, funny or serious. They spoke or sang their words in verses.

Actors performed on the circle of beaten earth called the *orchestra*. The theater at Epidauros (see page 9) could seat 12,000 spectators.

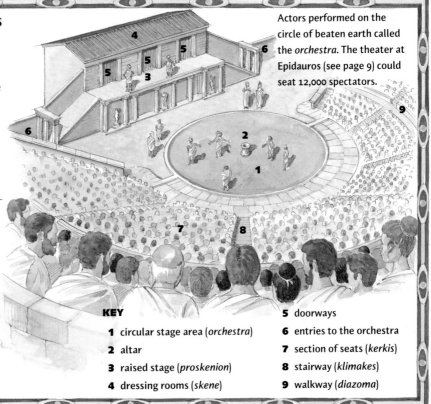

KEY

1 circular stage area (*orchestra*)
2 altar
3 raised stage (*proskenion*)
4 dressing rooms (*skene*)
5 doorways
6 entries to the orchestra
7 section of seats (*kerkis*)
8 stairway (*klimakes*)
9 walkway (*diazoma*)

Boxers wore leather thongs around their hands (like gloves).

The winner of the race in armor was proclaimed the 'Best of the Greeks'.

Winners at the Olympic Games were crowned with a garland of olive leaves.

THE END OF ANCIENT GREECE

There were many changes in Greece in the 300 years after the death of Alexander the Great. Not only was Alexander's empire divided among his generals, but the Romans from Italy grew so powerful that they eventually took control of Greece and all her lands. Greece was absorbed into the Roman Empire.

At its greatest extent, Alexander's empire stretched from Greece to India – a distance of 3,700 miles. This map shows how his empire was eventually split up into three Hellenistic kingdoms. Each kingdom was called after the general, or Successor, who first ruled there. ▶

ALEXANDER'S EMPIRE IS LOST

Within twenty years of Alexander's death in 323 BC, his great empire split up into smaller parts called 'kingdoms'. His generals, known as the Successors, fought among themselves for control of the kingdoms. Alexander's mother, wife, son and half-brother were all murdered in the struggle for power.

THE HELLENISTIC KINGDOMS

Alexander's empire eventually became three Hellenistic kingdoms. 'Hellenistic' comes from the Greek word *'Hellazein'*, which means 'to speak Greek or identify with the Greeks'. People in these kingdoms adopted a Greek way of life.

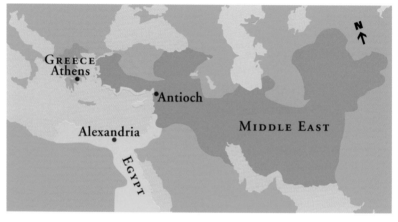

The Antigonid kingdom in Greece and Macedonia, first ruled by Antigonas

The Ptolemaic kingdom in Egypt, first ruled by Ptolemy

The Seleucid kingdom in the Middle East and beyond, first ruled by Seleucus

ALEXANDRIA

This city in the north of Egypt was founded by Alexander the Great. He was buried there in a golden coffin. Alexandria grew into a thriving city that was more Greek than Egyptian. It was sometimes called 'Alexandria-by-Egypt'. This let everyone know how different it was from other towns in Egypt. Under King Ptolemy I, Alexandria became the capital of Egypt and was more important even than Athens. The city's population of about 500,000 was a mix of Greeks, Egyptians, Jewish people and Orientals (people from countries in the East). Among its great buildings was the Library – the largest in the world. The Library contained thousands of papyrus scrolls, many of which were lost in a fire.

Rising to nearly 460 feet, the lighthouse at Alexandria was one of the Seven Wonders of the Ancient World. It was topped with a metal basket to hold its burning fire, and a statue of Zeus.

GREECE BECOMES PART OF THE ROMAN EMPIRE

The Romans came from Italy, a land to the west of Greece. First they took control of the Greek cities that had been built in southern Italy and Sicily (see page 10). Then the Romans turned their attention towards Greece and the lands of the Hellenistic kingdoms, all of which became part of the Roman Empire. The Romans liked many aspects of Greek culture. They adopted Greek ideas about architecture, literature and religion. This kept Greek culture alive. Even though the language of the Romans was Latin, not Greek, they used an alphabet based on the Greek alphabet. This is the one used today for English and most other European languages. Roman parents hired educated Greeks to teach their children.

GREEK GODS INTO ROMAN GODS

The Romans had a clever way of taking control of a country and its people. Whenever they found something they liked, they 'Romanized' it. This meant changing it to their way rather than destroying it. For example, the Romans began to worship the twelve Greek Olympian gods in their own religion. They changed the gods' names to Roman ones, but left their powers alone so that they would still be familiar to Greek people.

Aphrodite	**Apollo**	**Ares**	**Artemis**	**Athena**	**Demeter**
became	remained	became	became	became	became
Venus	**Apollo**	**Mars**	**Diana**	**Minerva**	**Ceres**

Dionysus	**Hephaestus**	**Hera**	**Hermes**	**Poseidon**	**Zeus**
became	became	became	became	became	became
Bacchus	**Vulcan**	**Juno**	**Mercury**	**Neptune**	**Jupiter**

SAILING INTO THE UNKNOWN

The spirit of adventure never seems to have left the Greeks, even though the world around them changed so much in the years after Alexander. In about 300 BC a Greek sailor called Pytheas, from the colony of Massalia (modern-day Marseille, in the south of France), explored the Atlantic coast in search of new trade routes. He claimed to have sailed around Britain and may have gone as far as Norway.

Pytheas saw something in which he could 'neither walk nor sail'. It was probably fog.

THE LAST YEARS OF ANCIENT GREECE AT A GLANCE

323 BC Death of Alexander the Great

307 BC Athens is captured by Antigonas, one of Alexander's generals

279 BC Greece is invaded by barbarian Gauls from the north

148 BC Macedonia becomes a province of Rome

146 BC Mainland Greece becomes a province of Rome

129 BC Greek cities overseas pass to the Romans

30 BC The Hellenistic Age ends

GLOSSARY

Acanthus A plant whose spiky leaves were carved on to buildings for decoration

Acropolis The name given to a hill at the heart of a Greek town

Agora An open space in a town center which served as market place, administrative center and social center

Barbarian Describing members of wild, uncivilized tribes

Barter When goods are exchanged for other goods without using money

Black-figure A style of pottery decoration with black figures on a red background

Capital The decorated top of a column

Caryatid Statue of a draped woman that took the place of a column

City-state A self-governing city and its land

Democracy Rule by many people

Flutes The vertical grooves that decorated columns

Hoplite A heavily-armed foot-soldier

Krater A large, deep pottery bowl

Marble A hard-wearing stone used for buildings and statues

Ostraka The Greek word for pieces of broken pottery used for voting

Papyrus A water reed from Egypt, used to make writing material of the same name

Pentathlon An athletic event of five different sports

Phalanx A war formation of hoplites

Red-figure A style of pottery decoration with red figures on a black background

Sarcophagus A coffin

Stoa A low building with columns along one side and shops inside

Trireme The main type of warship in the Greek navy

Volute Scroll-like decoration seen on some column capitals

INDEX